PLAN BASED

INVESTING

WHY A FINANCIAL PLAN IS THE KEY TO INVESTMENT SUCCESS

Jerry A. Ganz,
Certified Financial
Planner™

ISBN-10: 1482353466
EAN13: 9781482353464

Library of Congress Control Number: 2013903460
CreateSpace Independent Publishing Platform
North Charleston, South Carolina

Preface

Thirty years of working in the securities, tax, and insurance world has given me the opportunity to observe—to observe those who prioritize the future and those who do not. Those who don't eventually become those who do. Unfortunately, it is often much too late to make a significant difference.

The debate of what, when, and with whom is and will be constantly debated in the world of investing. Whom do we trust? What are the rules of achieving financial security? How do we invest? What are the best options? Are we on track to retire? Are the fees I am paying too high? Why am I paying fees at all? The world of finance is fraught with questions and opinions. There is no consensus on the right way to invest; there are theories, lots of them, but what is the best strategy?

This book is not about the best strategy, although I do touch on strategies. It is not about the proper level of fees, although I touch on fees. It is not about the rules of financial security, although I do touch on "rules." This book is about the proper what, when, why, and how to invest based on your Financial Plan. A plan for your money built backward from your dreams, converted to your goals, and then measured against your actual progress, it is called a "Financial Plan," and it is the key to success. I quote from the Bible's book of Luke: "Suppose one of you wants to build a tower. Won't you first sit down and estimate the cost to see if you have enough money to complete it?" It's interesting how the wisdom of over two thousand years ago still applies today and will tomorrow.

Let me ask you a similar question: if you plan to work forty to fifty years and then retire to live off of the money you set aside during those forty to fifty years for the balance of your life, doesn't it make sense to have a plan to do so? Doesn't it make sense to track your actual progress against that plan on a regular basis? Doesn't it make sense to choose your investments based on what your plan says your investments need to earn to accomplish your goals?

Welcome to *Plan-Based Investing*. This book is based on the simple yet extraordinary truth that it makes sense (a) to have a Financial Plan rather than not to have a plan, and (b) to use that plan to determine how you should invest. Are you able to build a home without a plan? Not if you are going to get the required permits. Are you able to invest in a 401(k) plan or with a broker or in an online seven dollar trading account without a plan? Absolutely you can. Is it a good idea? That is the basis of this book. Our industry—the financial services industry—is vast. We don't define the term *Advisor* very well, nor do we define *Financial Plan* very well. Therefore, we have a problem, and that problem is generation after generation of people getting shortchanged because they are receiving partial advice and think they are getting complete advice. You may think you are working with a Financial Planner on a Financial Plan, but since we don't agree on who or what that is, almost everything is permissible. That is a shame, and we are going to discuss that very dilemma in this book.

I spend a fair amount of time discussing financial disaster preparation in this book. The world is a different place in the 21st century than it was in the past. We have world economic problems (because we never had a plan—separate story). How will that economic disaster affect your life, your income, your debt—your plan? We can't know for sure, but we can prepare for what we do know are the possibilities.

The world's economy is in turmoil. For some reason the problem of spending more money than we have is not just confined to the United States. Countries around the world have done the same. Worse yet, we have made promises to millions of people to pay them Social Security and to subsidize their health insurance and pay them pensions when we don't have the money to do so. In Europe we have watched the Union of Countries demand of those in the worse shape to prescribe "austerity measures." These are cuts to the very programs they have come to rely upon. These are the same type of government benefits we have come to rely upon. The unions fight back saying they were promised benefits, but with no money, the promises can't be fulfilled. Can these countries survive this? No one is exactly sure. The United States is on the same path, as we as a country move forward with clear opposing goals of two political parties. The next "plan" is to get back into power and unwind the current plan. We avoid discussing a disaster plan or alternative plans as they are spun to show weakness or a lack of faith in your plan strategy. The truth is if you have built a Financial Plan without a disaster plan discussion, you need a new "Advisor." (Or you may need to fire the magazine, newspaper, or website that provides your advice.) These facts of governments around the world moving toward economic collapse are staring us all in the face. Not discussing them or their impact on your Financial Plan is, in my opinion, malpractice.

This book is not about the world's rapidly declining economic situation, *but* if you are not considering the impact of economic collapse and establishing a strategy to deal with such a decline, your plan and/or strategy is obsolete.

The world is different now than it has been for most of America's history, and common sense should tell us that we need to think differently about it.

I suggest that you design a Financial Plan—that Financial Plan will tell you what to do next, and it certainly will involve how you invest. I call it "Plan-Based Investing."

Questions and Answers

This question and answer section (Q&A) will help set the stage for the premise of Plan-Based Investing.

Q. Why?

A. In an interview, Dr. Michael Reizen, MD, notes that "Even if the pills are free in the VA and patients have hypertension and know that it is a serious disease, only one-third of those patients take the pills as prescribed—and that's when the pills are free! Only two-thirds even fill the prescription to start with." That sounds to me like failure. Why won't people do what is right for them? I don't know. (*Creating Trust* by Matt Zagula and Dan S. Kennedy)

Statistics for people who start working at age twenty-five by the time they are age sixty-five:

- One percent are considered wealthy.
- Four percent have adequate capital stowed away for retirement.
- Sixty-three percent are dependent on Social Security, friends, relatives, or charity.

That sounds to me like failure. Why don't people save more money? Why don't they control their spending? Why won't they...? All great questions, with no one answer. My theory is that a Financial Plan is a part of the answer. It will outline goals, it will track your progress, and it will point you to how to invest. That is Plan-Based Investing.

Q. What is the premise of Plan-Based Investing?

A. Investing is a way to increase the chances of accomplishing a goal. Without goals you won't have a plan. A "Financial Plan" is a written outline and strategy of converting dreams to goals, with a plan to achieve them and a tracking method to follow your progress and make adjustments.

The chicken and the egg analogy is a core to the Plan-Based Investing strategy. Should we invest and live with the results, or should we decide on the results we want and invest accordingly to accomplish those goals? Here's a quick test for you to consider which camp your Advisor is in. At your last review meeting did you discuss the returns of your investments or the return on your investments as they relate to your Financial Plan?

Q. Doesn't my "Advisor" handle that?

A.   Maybe. In my experience, the world of investment brokerage has a different methodology in how they do business. Their goal in many ways is to first determine your ability to tolerate a drop in your portfolio value. Brokers utilize a "risk questionnaire" of some sort to help them with this process. Once the series of questions determines where you are uncomfortable and likely to panic, they recommend a slight backup in risk, meaning they back off on the aggressiveness of the portfolio to the point where you will hang in there and not panic and sell. You should then invest with this newfound "risk-adjusted portfolio" and plod forward.

Once your Advisor has a written record of your risk questionnaire results and has assigned those results to an allocation mix, he or she can now defend himself or herself against the force of the law as he or she has followed industry standard practice.

Q. Why is that so bad?

A.   It's simple: the odds that your risk-tolerance comfort level and the mix of investments will match the savings rate must have some long odds. The truth is most people don't outline their dreams and establish goals to accomplish them. This strategy—or lack of strategy—leads to settling for whatever you get in the end. Doesn't it make more sense to define your dreams, translate them into goals, and build a plan to accomplish them?

Q. What if I need to take a higher risk with my investments than I am comfortable with?

Taking on more risk than one is comfortable with is seldom the only choice. Honestly, it is the course of choice because you have no desire to sacrifice lifestyle. You may have to sacrifice to save more money or sacrifice your need for income in retirement because of your lifestyle choice. This can take on the form of reduced spending and/or additional employment to and through retirement to make that happen. If you need to take on more risk than you are comfortable with, you need to be aware of this, and you need to fully commit to your goals. (I am referring to market risk. More on risks in chapter 4.) If you need a return greater than the historic return of the investments you are investing in, then you are in trouble. I want to say that again. If you need a return greater than the historic return of the investments you are investing in, then you are in trouble. You are expecting an investment to perform in excess of its historic norm. Does this not sound insane? Unfortunately, far too many people don't know what rate of return they need over time. Plan-Based Investing is about the process of completing a Financial Plan and using it to determine that rate of return and then how to invest.

You may now be getting a glimpse of why Advisors don't complete Financial Plans for their clients. They would then be held accountable to provide and monitor strategies to achieve them.

Q. So how is Plan-Based Investing different from the traditional investment advice?

A. In Plan-Based Investing, you have a real Financial Plan and you *monitor it regularly, comparing* your current standing to the goals that need to be met to provide a lifetime of retirement income and/ or other goals that you have established. You know how to invest because you know what your investments need to do to complete your plan.

Note: The lower the investment returns you need to accomplish your goals the greater the likelihood of accomplishing them. Think about that a minute—it is profound. If you need a 12 percent return to accomplish your plan, you have a problem. If a 5 percent return will accomplish your goals, your odds of reaching your goals have greatly improved. A 5 percent return is just easier to accomplish year in and year out than a 12 percent return.

Q. You make it sound as if this is *not* a "do-it-yourself" program—is that right?

A. The fact is many investors need help protecting themselves from themselves. (Honestly, so do a lot of so-called Advisors.) Left alone, we will justify failed goals as bad luck and lower our goals to set up the opportunity to meet our new goals. Adjusting goals downward is a quick and easy indicator of either unrealistic goals or a poor strategy to accomplish those goals. An unbiased Advisor can help you determine which of the two it was and establish a new track to success.

Failed goals are a fact of life, no investment is perfect, life's timing sometimes sucks, health is undependable, and so on. Financial Planning is financial strategizing. A partner in this process to keep you accountable to your goals should bring value beyond his or her cost.

Advice takes on two forms: opinion and counsel. Those who understand success in our society will entertain your opinion at a cocktail party, but when it comes to wise decisions, they seek counsel. Counsel is provided by people with experience, knowledge, and wisdom. Determining which of the two you are getting is a starting point to a successful outcome.

GREAT POINT (GP) #1: "Advice" without accountability is opinion. Don't stake your future on opinion.

Q. How does this distinction change the concept of Financial Planning?

A. It doesn't. The art and practice of Financial Planning is very well defined by the College of Financial Planning (www.cfp.net). The college has rigid standards with a common problem—how do you hold everyone with the CFP® credentials to that standard? What about those without the CFP® credentials?

Plan-Based Investing is taking the proven process to the next level by exposing the fact that those who shortcut the process are shortchanging you. If you don't have a Financial Plan, you need one. If you are not using your Financial Plan to determine how to invest, you have been shortchanged with an incomplete plan. Seriously, how can you be sure of what to do next if you don't have a plan?

Q. Won't the Financial Planning industry embrace this concept?

A. Unlikely. Advisors measure success with a measurement of "assets under management" or AUM. Insurance professionals measure success with the value of annual premiums written. Doesn't it make more sense to measure how many Financial Plans have been implemented that are or were successful? The industry doesn't and won't.

Unfortunately, the problems with the Financial Planning industry are far fewer than the problems with the accepted advice-providers of modern times. They are the mega-mutual fund or ETF sponsors or the financial pornography publications. (*Mega fund* is my reference to the large mutual fund outlets that work very hard to defend their industry. *ETF* is an acronym for exchange traded funds, which trade many indices as if they were stocks. Their claim to fame is that they provide a large amount of diversification at a low cost and with intraday trading versus mutual funds, which normally have higher fees and trade at the end of the day after the stock market has closed. The largest ETF at this time is "SPY," which invests in the same assets in the same ratio of the S&P 500® Index. *Financial pornography* is my short name for the financial publications that sell with big headlines and big promises with *no accountability* because they provide only broad-based advice.) These outlets of advice have brainwashed the public into focusing only on fees and "hot trends." You may know them as *Money®* as a magazine publication, the *Wall Street Journal®* as a newspaper, or Bloomberg Television® as a TV station. I have nothing against these outlets of information; my issue is with the headlines that they use to sell and how they provide an advertising platform for investment managers who seldom if ever believe it is a bad time to invest in what they sell.

Q. Are there investments that should always be avoided?

A. Competition for your dollars is a vicious fight carried out every day between banks, mutual fund companies, stock markets, insurance companies, landowners, real estate agents, and hundreds of other options for how and where you invest your money. Every investment has its own risks and potential return. Just like the way politicians can spin what you said to mean something else, Advisors can spin your current investments as bad and their recommendations as better. The point of this book is not to compare investments; it is to say that if they are sold to you without the motive of completing your Financial Plan, you don't know whether they are good or bad. The point of Plan-Based Investing is to utilize investments that will move you toward the completion of your personal Financial Plan.

Q. Is Plan-Based Investing as easy as it sounds?

A.   Plan-Based Investing takes work. It involves establishing a real Financial Plan with real goals, set to a real time frame. It involves updates to data and regular comparisons to your "goal progress status. For many, if not most, people it involves working with a Financial Advisor who is compensated enough to provide these services and to schedule regular time for you.

Q&A Conclusion:

The Financial services industry has failed to increase the financial intelligence of this country. Much like the government, we continue to perpetuate failed strategies because we have the hope that the results will be better. I believe Plan-Based Investing is common sense, and I pray that this book expresses it in a way that strikes you as common sense too. Although there are many paths to success, most of us work very hard and don't take the time to design, implement, and monitor a Financial Plan. Part of the reason I wrote this book is that I understand that people need help to develop and follow such a plan. My hope with this book is that you will accept the Plan-Based Investing strategy and seek out a trusted Advisor to partner with you to move you forward to success.

Thank You

Dan Kennedy, from the world of Glazer-Kennedy, motivated me to write my business strategy and business philosophy in this book. If you are a business owner, you would do well to seek him out.

Learn more about Kennedy at www.dankennedy.com.

Brian Tracy has authored a truckload of books. Start with *Goals*, but have your pen and paper ready to make notes and form action plans. Learn more about Brian at www.briantracy.com.

Thanks, guys! My life has been changed because of you!

My primary mentors were my parents. Jerrold "Baldy" and Sally Ganz are two of the hardest working people I have ever met. Their life experiences were priceless to me. I learned from them that if you never take risks, you never experience all the growth potential in your life. They were willing to take the risk, and my siblings and I benefited from the blessings of that courage. My parents have never stopped charging forward. They have and will sacrifice everything they have for their children. My wife, Debbie, is cut from that same cloth. There is no sacrifice greater than for our children, Brittany, Keil, Spencer and Miles. For that I am eternally grateful and forever indebted to each of them.

Thank You Paul Goderstad for his art work which was developed into the book's cover. Paul is an incredible talent and far too modest about his gift.

Table of Contents

The Concept

The concepts that make up Plan-Based Investing are not just about why you need a Financial Plan—there is no shortage of reasons why a written Financial Plan improves results. Instead, they address the silly notions that anything other than your Financial Plan should determine how you invest. Primary among such notions are your "risk tolerance" and your age. They are silly because the "securities industry" is programmed to defend itself against lawsuits and large "investment account" losses versus failed goals. The risk tolerance questionnaire, which most of us have filled out once upon a time, is the tool that allows the securities industry to defend itself against account losses. **Plan-Based Investing** is the overall strategy that says the "planning community" should defend itself against failed goals rather than matching your risk tolerance to a properly blended portfolio of investments or choosing a portfolio mix because of your age. Unfortunately, far too many Advisors are trained to sell products, not design Financial Plans. That's a shame, and while the world focuses on the lowest fees, they forget that far too many people haven't even started saving yet. (Please note that an Advisor can be a broker, a website, an insurance agent, or any number of others who practice investment management.)

GP #2: Let me give you some insight on fees. You may try to negotiate the advisor fee down thinking you are saving money, when the reality is you are moving down his or her priority list because there are others willing to pay for superior service and to obtain superior results. Be careful with fees so that you understand when they are or are not appropriate.

Plan-Based Investing is a new approach identified by its name. You don't simply match a set of investments to your risk comfort level. You need to build *your* Financial Plan and decide what return will achieve your goals considering savings rate, taxation, inflation, and time. Understand that "plan" in this context may sound as if it is a one-time event, but a Financial Plan is really a financial strategy that will need to be tweaked and adjusted throughout your life. The world and success in it are moving targets; your life's goals will change because your dreams will change. That fact gives fuel to the fire for the "make as much money as you can crowd" that leads to stress beyond what you need in your life. A secret to life is to minimize stress, and a Financial Plan will lower stress in direct proportion to how early in life you prepare one.

The current system of Financial Planning, as I will expose it, is filled with shortcomings. Those in the lower and middle classes in our country are underserved by the planning community and are easy targets for salesmen willing to unload the "product of choice" as a "fix all." Most in need of planning are seldom convinced of its value, and if convinced they are unable to find a qualified planner willing to do the planning for a fee at a rate they consider reasonable. (I do not have a great solution for this problem. The people with the least amount of money have the need for a large amount of advice. Unfortunately, this is where people become addicted to "financial pornography"—outlets that provide "unaccountable advice" for your subscription of $14.95 a year.)

Financial Planning is not a product or a strategy. It is a historically tried and tested process. Plan-Based Investing is a lifestyle of designing, implementing, tracking, and monitoring progress toward an end. The end is often **Plan-Based Estate Planning** and will be covered in a future book. It is a relationship with a competent planning professional who is committed to his or her trade and its professional code of conduct. The professional designations in the industry are numerous and growing. A professional designation is an indicator of a completed field of study for which the certification is earned. These designations include the Certified Financial Planner™, the designation I have earned. (Note: There is a bucket load of "designations," and none of them is a guarantee of competence.) These designations also do not indicate the type of practice that the Advisor is operating and many times are used to sell products with an implied level of expertise. (The CFP® and CHFC® are two of the older, most respected designations and require a rigorous qualification.) Caution: There is no one way to financial success, *but* "a plan" has been accepted in society as a requirement for everything from building permits to business loans. It is time that society embraces the benefits of owning up to the future by establishing that we are all on a financial path, and we will all benefit greatly by knowing the path we are on and then planning for the outcome we desire.

Wisdom to Ponder:

Desperate people will believe outrageous promises.

"Why, sometimes I've believed as many as six impossible things before breakfast."
–Lewis Carroll, Alice in Wonderland

GP #3: There is no guarantee for success. Designing, implementing, and monitoring a Plan-Based Investing strategy will provide you with the knowledge to understand where you stand today in the pursuit of your goals.

GP #4: People get crapped on. We will always have poor citizens in our country. Over two thousand years ago Jesus was recorded in Matthew 12:8 as saying, "You will always have the poor among you, but you will not always have me." How we lift these citizens up is how our society will be measured by history.

A "Plan-Based" lifestyle provides hope for individuals the same way maps (or GPS for you younger folks) provide hope for us to reach our destination. If you understand that logic, you can then separate yourself from the crowd and act on building your new "Plan-Based" lifestyle.

Let me introduce you to our sample couple Ralph and Lorraine. They have 2.2 children in high school, they both work, and they are "good savers." With Lorraine's recent bonus they find themselves with excess money they are not accustomed to having. They now want to know what to do next. Should they increase the funding to their 401(k)s, in the tax-deductible 401(k) or the Roth 401(k)? Is it better if they invest in their own IRAs or Roth IRAs? Are they eligible? What about college costs?

Solution: a Plan. As an experienced Advisor I could defend a variety of solutions to Ralph and Lorraine's dilemmas. They have a surplus of cash, and determining how to invest it will involve a thorough review of their goals and philosophies. (Example: How much of their children's college costs do they plan to pay, if any?) Plan-Based Investing is as much about the titling of the accounts as to how it is invested. Roth IRA and Roth 401(k) sound similar but are miles apart as they relate to paying college costs for your children.

There's more to come about Ralph and Lorraine and their Financial Planning challenges later in the book.

CHAPTER ONE

In the Beginning...

In the beginning God had a plan, and it was foiled by the greed and desire for something not needed. Surrounded by perfection, those two people were convinced that they needed something they didn't have.

Lesson one: Plans are foiled continuously.

We make plans daily—where and when mostly, but for many they include the details of an agenda along with expected outcomes. Some are written, some are recorded as an audio reminder, and others are committed to mental storage. The capacity of that mental storage is limited directly by the amount of information you have committed to it, your surroundings, various distractions and the timing of those distractions, age, and personal prioritization.

Multitasking, an attribute often assigned only to women, is actually a daily necessity. Most of us need to walk and chew gum if we want to go anywhere while we are enjoying our gum. We need to talk, dictate, or text while we travel, and if we are not yet twenty-five years old, we complete homework in front of a TV with a remote to avoid commercial slowdowns and our phone at the ready for texting and Facebook viewing. The problem never is or has been our ability to multitask; it is to know which tasks to complete and to complete the tasks that move us forward toward our goals.

"Plan B" is a term associated with the change of direction we must make if and when our initial greatest and most preferred plan runs into insurmountable roadblocks.

Lesson two: Plan B may be the preferred plan yet untested—it is certainly preferred to failure.

The goal of this book is to convince you of the value of a Plan-Based Investing strategy and of a written Financial Plan. It is to encourage you to quantify your dreams—to make them goals—and to establish a lifetime goal and tracking system to check your progress to accomplish them. The Plan B's will be continuous as you hit obstacles and, more importantly, as you change, update, and broaden or narrow your goals.

Lesson three: Downsized goals are often the indication of a failed plan.

Goals reduced and/or time frames extended are a result of fairy-tale goals or dreams never put in writing and that, therefore, never became real goals. They never had a chance because you never created a workable plan, and you didn't share that plan with an accountability partner. *Let me give you an example. Did you ever say to friends at any time in your twenties or thirties that you were going to retire by the time you were fifty? Why didn't that happen? I would guess that if you are like me, you failed because you never designed a plan to accomplish that goal. You could argue that it was never a goal, but rather a dream. I believe that we seldom get what we dream of; instead, we get what we plan for.* Today is the day you *learn the key to success* that can change your life forever.

Chapter Two

Rules of Thumb

Rules of thumb have been used since the beginning of time to explain things. Today they have evolved into shortcuts used to justify a point. A rule of thumb is often presented in association with a rule of thumb that you have come to expect in your mind as true, implying that both are true. Let me give you an example of a salesperson using two rules of thumb to convince you of the soundness of them to forward their point. "The proper level of stock exposure in your portfolio can be figured by subtracting your age from one hundred and ten. This is a rule of thumb like the rule of thumb that says you should use a dime-size spot of shampoo in the palm of your hand to wash your hair." Since that rule about shampoo sounds sensible, you assume that the rule of thumb about the level of stock market exposure is also correct.

Here are some examples of common "rules of thumb" in the investment world:

"Save an amount equal to twenty-five times your annual earnings."

"Ten times earnings is all the life insurance you need."

"Eighty percent of your current pay is all you will need in retirement."

Rules of thumb are used in all areas of life continuously by the "lack of accountability" crowd and are often found in sources like these:

- magazines with headlines to sell solutions to complex problems with "quick and easy" ideas
- competitive sales strategies to validate claims they are making

- College courses taught by "know-it-alls" to minimize the need for professional help and elevate their status as a knowledge source
- anyone *not intelligent enough or unwilling to* actually do the research to determine the correct strategy for you

Lesson four: *Rules of thumb are guidelines. Only an idiot believes they are rules to base your life's goals on. We are all unique, so our Financial Plan should be unique. Rules of thumb are the opposite of personalized advice.*

Lesson five: *If everything worthwhile were quick and easy, we wouldn't live in a country with roughly 15 percent of the population on food assistance subsidies each week! (Fifteen percent of three hundred million is mind-boggling!)*

The advantage of living in the twenty-first century—beyond all of the technological advances, all of the communication options, and all of the travel options—is *personalization.* We can get our name on just about anything; we can program almost any electronic gadget to our own user preferences. Successful *marketers know that anything they can personalize creates an attachment beyond the value of just ownership.* Yet we settle for rules of thumb, the direct opposite of personalization. Financial pornography publications and news sources that sell with big flashy headlines need rules of thumb because they cannot provide personal advice. The idea is to sell themselves as a trusted source of information, and they need to appeal to as mass an audience as possible to make this a reality.

I would recommend that you consider rules of thumb as a starting point with your planning and not a goal. There are Financial Planning experts available today who can and will provide personalized advice for you. In my experience not everything is as simple as it is described, and therefore few complex problems can be solved with simple solutions. Program yourself to be alert when you hear the words "rule of thumb" and consider them a shortcut of advice rather than personalized advice.

The most common rule of thumb that I see is that because you are saving "what you can afford," everything will be OK. I also hear it said that when clients are saving 10 percent of their income, they believe they must be on track toward a successful retirement. The world does not owe you a comfortable retirement. Your employer does not owe you a successful retirement. The government does not owe you a successful retirement. You owe yourself a successful retirement. A Financial Plan is a strategy to make that happen.

Let's get back to Ralph and Lorraine, the couple you were introduced to in the opening of the book. In our last scenario Lorraine received a sizeable bonus. How does her scenario change if she received a sizeable bonus but now needs to cover the full cost of her health insurance? She was investing 7 percent of her pay in her 401(k) and is receiving a 3 percent match on those contributions, giving her the 10 percent savings she was told to set as a goal. How does the new health insurance premium affect her 401(k) savings strategy? Is there a better way to pay it? What are the alternatives with and without the cooperation of her employer? Does it change the allocation she needs to contribute to her 401(k)?

The last question is a trick question and a test to see if you are paying attention. Lorraine is *investing* at a gross rate of 10 percent, which is a rule of thumb, not a *savings* rate that has been checked against her goals. The idea of Plan-Based Investing is to know how much to invest and where to invest it, and then to check it against the goals moving forward.

CHAPTER THREE

What Is a "Financial Plan"?

Analogy: Call up tens of thousands of military personnel aboard battleships along with fully stocked aircraft carriers, tanks, helicopters, planes, and assorted weaponry to destroy the enemy. You arrive and the enemy is gone—they moved. Would anyone undertake such a large event without advanced pre-engagement intelligence, a goal, a strategy, and a plan? Yet people move forward in their lives without the same level of advanced planning, and they and their families' futures are at stake.

Next time?

The US military is an example of strategic planning to the *n*th degree. Soldiers study, train, and prepare for adversity and then prepare for the specific details of the mission. They know their roles and know them to perfection, and when the "curveballs" of military action occur, they are prepared and are ready to adapt and change to overcome. Their motivation? There may not be a next time.

You save money every month in your 401(k) at work, put in a full week of work, and own insurance to protect your family if you die or become disabled. You buy a home the bank says you can afford, you buy a car every five to seven years, and you lease a second to project the right image—yes, you have a plan! Yes, Mr. and/or Mrs. Average American, you have a "plan"—a "plan" that has as great a chance of success as the next guy's. After all, you can't help it if your wages freeze for four years or if a new job opportunity comes along and you withdraw the $6,000 in your 401(k) to pay down your student loans. It happens to everyone. Doesn't it?

Lesson six: *Your Financial Plan is a personal plan. It is* your *Financial Plan and cannot be compared to anyone else's through normal visual means.*

A Financial Plan can be thought of as a road map or an instruction manual. It is built based on your goals, which are converted to monitored checkpoints that you monitor while moving toward the end goal. If the goal is a comfortable retirement, it will require a certain amount of savings. It would make sense that we save in an efficient way, and it would also seem logical to use investments that provide the greatest chance of success whether or not the stock market, bond market, real estate market, or interest rates are willing to cooperate.

The world is a movie. Sets are assembled or purchased, and we, the actors, learn our roles. We are an outward success with big homes, new cars, great clothes, frequent-flier miles, and expensive toys, living the "American Dream." Our daily movie is created and the script tweaked to make us look like we belong, or better yet, like we are leading the charge in the "New Economy." We compare ourselves and our success to our peers, who are also creating and tweaking their movie scripts based on their fantasy island and not on reality.

We grade on a curve; we look around and compare. We denigrate those with more as taking an unfair advantage or just being lucky. We don't understand how the Joneses can afford a boat and a snowmobile, but, heck, at least our boat is bigger than theirs. Yes, we grade on a curve, and worse yet *we compare ourselves to something not real.* We compare to their movie. The actors in their movie are good. They play their parts daily and seldom are seen out of character. They themselves don't know reality anymore. They certainly don't want to be exposed by a Financial Plan.

Lesson seven: *Maturity is honesty, being honest about where you are in relation to where you should be toward the accomplishment of your dreams. You can't honestly assess where you are going if you can't honestly determine where you stand today.*

The movie plays on, and enough people seem to have their lives worked out just fine. You are following the masses. You read the smart magazine articles and the financial newspapers. Hey, you even read the book that the company gave you with your 401(k) enrollment. Based on these actions, you convince yourself you are just fine.

Wake up—a Financial Plan will either verify that you are or you aren't!

What a Financial Plan Isn't

A Financial Plan is not universally accepted as just one thing. It varies as to what it is by who is telling you what it is.

Lesson eight: *A "Financial Plan" can be any plan related to finances, complete or not. It can also be created by anyone. That is not good.*

Lesson nine: *If the financial industry cannot define what an Advisor is, it certainly can't define what a Financial Plan is. So caveat emptor (buyer beware) when preparing or purchasing a Financial Plan.*

A Financial Plan is not strictly any of the following:

- an investment strategy (most often confused with a Financial Plan)
- an insurance strategy
- a cash-flow strategy
- an estate-transfer strategy
- a tax strategy

You know this, yet millions of you don't take the initiative to explore the benefits of having all of those issues addressed in a written plan of action and goal comparison. You know the greatest military in the history of the world is the US military when it has a clear objective and permission to win. The level of detail in its planning is second to none. That is certainly the reason for its success and for our confidence in future successes. Its "plan" and "planning process" are proven, repeated over and over again and "personalized" to the situation.

The basics of a written Financial Plan are also known by you and nearly every clear-thinking American today.

- You need a "Cash Flow" statement (budget).
- You need a "Balance Sheet" and to know your "Net Worth" (where you are today).
- You need to define your dreams, convert them to goals, and establish a plan to achieve them.
- You need to use the "Cash Flow," "Balance Sheet," and "Net Worth" statements to compare your progress to your "Written Financial Plan."
- You need to revise the plan regularly to your changing dreams.

Lesson ten: *The premise of Plan-Based Investing is to determine what investments and investment strategies to use based on your Financial Plan. If just about anything written by anyone can be considered a Financial Plan, you can see where we may have some problems. Minimum criteria are necessary for a Financial Plan to be considered thorough enough to be used to initiate your Plan-Based Investing strategy. I recommend you review the five items listed above and consider them to be a base minimum.*

Let me tell you a short story about a couple I met years ago. As I often do, I asked them to bring along their Financial Plan when they came in to visit me. What they brought along was a large binder filled with page upon page of what they called their Financial Plan. They did not use it; as a matter of fact, they had never referred to it since it was created by their former Advisor. The information was good, but the premise of the plan was to sell them mutual funds, in which they invested. It was a sales tactic; it was not a Financial Plan to be reviewed or to have their investment progress measured against.

That is wrong, and yet you could make an argument that what they did was Plan-Based Investing. You should now be able to see that the concept of Plan-Based Investing is not a sound theory if the Financial Plan is poorly designed or was prepared to sell you investments or insurance versus fulfilling your financial goals.

CHAPTER FOUR

The Risks You Thought You Knew and Some You Didn't Think Of

Subtitle: If you have not been convinced that a Plan-Based Investing strategy is a wise strategy, maybe I can show you a little truth about the world today to move you to action.

Lesson Eleven: *A "risk philosophy" is an overall bias that we and/or our Advisor has that limits or protects us.*

Risk protection limits us if the risk never materializes and we lose our risk premium. Looking back we will be able to defend the limits and/or the protection and determine whether it was worth it. (This is a bit sarcastic but a truism nonetheless.) "Peace of mind" is hard to quantify. It is a by-product of proper risk management and is a benefit to you today.

Risk is most often discussed in the terms of loss. This book is not intended to be one of academic reference but a guide to success and dream accomplishment.

That said, have you considered the following risks?

> **Property and casualty risk.** You need to insure against loss that will adversely affect your Financial Plan at a level commensurate with the assets you need to protect and the liquid assets you have available to replace or repair them.

Income risk. If the income doesn't come in, who is dependent on it? This income production needs to be protected against destruction and failure (for instance, death and disability).

Retirement-income risk. If income is not adequate to cover expenses, one of two adjustments will need to be made: reduction in the reliance on the income or creation of more income. Protection against this risk is a Financial Plan, a miracle, an inheritance, lottery winnings, or upward mobility with a lifetime partner with greater wealth than yours. I am advocating a Financial Plan. Each of the others comes with its own inherent risks that space does not allow me to expand on further.

Inflation risk. The risk of inflation is the risk that costs will rise beyond what you planned and compensated for (i.e., your purchasing power declines). This risk is common to herd-mentality groups that have a normalcy bias that the future will repeat what the past has shown us. (A normalcy bias is an extremely limiting outlook that does not allow one to consider that the future could present scenarios or obstacles that vary widely from current estimates of what constitutes "normal.")

Normalcy-bias risk. This is a thought pattern that says life is and always will be within "normal" parameters, so preparation for new risks is not necessary. For example, a person might think it is normal to be healthy; therefore, he or she does not consider not being healthy for an extended period of time. This logical fallacy is often used to justify not planning at all. It is critical to prepare for life's curveballs; life will not unfold as you planned it. In *Leadership*, Rudy Giuliani wrote, "We did not anticipate that airliners would be commandeered and turned into guided missiles; but the fact that we practiced for other kinds of disasters made us far more prepared to handle a catastrophe that nobody envisioned." If you and your Advisor have never discussed what you will do in the event of a disaster that will affect your investments, is it because you not understand normalcy-bias risk?)

We all suffer from a normalcy bias; it is our natural tendency when someone shares with you risks that are not a part of what you consider to be "normal." We may laugh at it, make light of it, ignore it, or attack the deliverer of the information as "out of the mainstream." I can assure you that I am very "normal" and also rather inquisitive and untrusting of "normal."

"Everyone experienced the same thing" risk. This is a second cousin to normalcy-bias risk, where we are able to justify setbacks that we think are happening to everyone. For example, a person might reason that he or she's investment portfolio was down 42 percent in 2008, but so was everyone's. Or a person might think, I lost my home in the flood, but so did the entire town. This reasoning is a great cover-up for failed advanced planning.

Financial-pornography risk. This term refers to the idea that reading or watching and accepting advice given en masse without liability to the provider of the information will be a benefit to you and worthy of following. This rampant risk desires to change the argument to anything other than success and accountability. By its nature it is given with a disclaimer to protect the provider of the information. An example is "five investments everyone should have in their portfolio."

Selfish-advice risk. This risk is often very hard to detect. It is a risk that the advice you receive is being given out of the self-interest and improvement of the advice giver beyond what is fair. (I am not going to discuss "fair" because it is a minefield of opinions.) This risk exists in every situation where advice is given in lesser or greater degree. For example, an Advisor might say that a customer doesn't want to buy a bond because his or her CDs are backed by the FDIC or perhaps that other firms' fees are higher, without any discussion of value for fees. It is the motive of all providers of information to prop up a person's opinion of that provider of the information. While it will always exist, you overlook selfish advice if you feel you can trust your advice provider. (Hopefully by the end of this book you will change your feelings from just "trusting your advice giver" to "trusting your advice giver with the accomplishment of your goals.")

Intelligent leadership risk. This risk is a belief that individuals in leadership roles are smarter than the rest of us and know what is going on. This issue is complex and must be considered on a company-by-company and individual-by-individual basis. (Believing in intelligent leadership is a bad assumption.) An example as it applies to investment planning is that some investment companies provide titles to their Advisors that assume a level of competence.

Financial prediction risk. This is another common risk in which one's decisions are based on the predictions of coming events or trends. Predictions are nearly always correct, but the timing of them can vary greatly and tend to be modified to fit the prediction. This risk is easy to spot on daily, televised business programs. Believing in the art of market timing is a bold example of this risk. Market timing is the fool's gold of Plan-Based Investing.

Fantasy-life risk. This is the risk of assuming that everyone else is doing fine, and you are the only one who struggles with financial shortfalls. It is common if your friends and family are good actors and/or you watch too many feel-good movies or TV shows.

"No-load" risk, otherwise known as "low-fee" risk. This is the risk that the cost of your planning is the primary consideration of the decisions you make in regard to your Financial Plan. This is a common risk in which advice is given en masse versus personalized advice. It is often used as an argument changer. If you can't talk about what should be important to families (goal accomplishment), you change the argument to your strength—low fees.

Lower-fee risk. This entails the risk of making a change because of a fee that is lower than the one you are currently paying. This argument is often used as motivation to refinance a loan, reposition assets to another custodian, change life insurance policies, or change tax preparers or preparer software. Similar to low-fee risk, it is often prescribed without a discussion on value provided.

Sell-timing risk. It is never the time to sell. Either the value is down and one can't sell a loser, or it is high and will certainly go higher. This risk is a common one to individuals without a Plan-Based Investing strategy that provides a reference as to a total return needed to reach your goals.

Loyalty risk. It has always been good; therefore, it always will be good. Refer also to normalcy bias.

Broker risk. This is expecting biased advice from someone who will not get paid unless he sells you something. Earning a living or getting rich are not inherently unworthy goals as long as they are not done at the expense of others who suffer from the sale due to excessive charges. All relationships in your life should be based on win-win, and that includes your relationship with your Financial Advisor.

Headline Risk. Do you dig deep into a story or read the headline and think you have the overall gist of the article? Heads up—many article authors don't write their own headlines. The publication does that. Forget about the bias of the author; just think about you having a few minutes and skimming the newspaper in the morning.

Negative/positive short-term feeling risk. Believe it or not, your long-term decision making is influenced by the short-term news. My guess is that if you left an Anthony Robbins seminar, you would be more inclined to "go long" (bet on the market going up). If the stock market suffers a major decline, are you inclined to believe it is a trend or a buying opportunity?

Advisor-optimism risk. You don't pay an Advisor to be an optimist. You pay him or her to be a realist.

Gold-commercials risk. This is the risk that you believe every day is a good day to buy gold.

You-don't-need-anyone-else risk. This risk is believing that your Advisor is so smart that you don't need anyone else to help with your plan. He or she is a one-stop shop.

Lost opportunity risk. This risk is the "coulda, woulda, shoulda" missed opportunity story we all have. It starts with "I wish I would have bought _____ when it was at _____ (a level significantly lower than the current level). The truth is if you don't have a savings/opportunity account with money available to take advantage of the opportunity, you didn't miss it at all. Looking back at history is the only time you can justify borrowing to invest. (That is sarcasm.) Your Financial Plan and its success are not determined by your missed opportunities, but by what you learned from missing it and by what you plan to do going forward.

American mentality risk. We in America have a tendency to save to spend. We justify spending our savings versus taking out a loan—but then forget to continue the savings habit. You have heard all your life to "pay yourself first." That means to make savings a priority. Part of Plan-Based Investing is "plan on saving."

The next chapter continues with the disclosure of risks that relate to the coming economic unrest for America that has already begun to rear its ugly head around the world.

Expanded Risk Discussion from a Worldwide Economic Perspective

These newly identified risks relate to our country's financial condition and how that condition will relate to *your* Financial Plan. Numerous risks we all face will have a significant impact on your planning success. At the top of this list is the scam put forth by government officials all over the world, including the country in which I live, the United States. The risk of a collapse of our system is real, and our leaders' unwillingness to help us face up to the cost to fix this problem is a scam of epic proportions.

This financial disaster will affect everything we have grown to trust and believe in. I draw an analogy with your own family. If your fiscal scale is out of balance, meaning your income will not cover your living expenses and savings needs, then you are on a path toward problems. The deficit may be short-term in nature or it may be the beginning of a long-term shortfall. If you don't bring in enough income, you must cut expenses or tap into savings. If you don't, you will either need to sell your belongings to make up the shortfall, or someone will take them from you. If you can borrow money to cover the shortfall, that is a short-term, stopgap measure. If you lose your creditworthiness, you will need to borrow at higher interest rates, which will exacerbate the problem due to higher payments on the higher-rate loans. If you are able to manipulate the interest rates charged on your loans, you can certainly delay the crisis date, but you can't avoid it.

What if you borrow from your retirement savings for current expenses? That will definitely get you through today, but you have done so while compromising your retirement.

What if you file bankruptcy and walk away? Then you transfer your problem to others who trusted you to repay. If the debt forgiven is large enough, it can cause a failure of the institution that trusted you to repay it.

I hope you can understand those comments as they relate to our government. Our governments, including federal and many state and local governments, are spending more than they receive in tax and fee revenue. In the case of the federal government, it has used the money from our retirement system, Social Security, with the promise to pay it back. The truth of debt repayment is that when it is time to pay it back, you need to lower payments in another area of your budget or increase your income or some combination of both. In the case of the United States government, what are we going to cut? What history do we have as a nation in cutting expenses? That is a problem.

Answering this problem requires no studies or research. We all know it. We are living beyond our means, and we have done so for many years. Our unwillingness to change this behavior will lead to destruction, and we will all be to blame by not holding our leaders accountable. Here are some of the risks we face:

> **Social Security–reduction risk.** This risk is that ultimately Social Security payments will either need to be reduced or the rate of increase will be stopped or slowed. The unwillingness to attack the issue of an underfunded system by putting reduced benefits in place for future generations is unforgivable. (A Ponzi scheme is defined as telling someone he or she is paying for one thing when his or her money is being used for something else, and, yes, the term applies to Social Security.)

> **Reduced-pension risk.** This risk is identical to the risk with Social Security. Past benefit calculations were a sham. There is not enough money to pay all of the pension obligations that have been made. The problem, as with most underfunding problems, is that the longer we delay corrective actions, the less we are able to compensate for those reductions in our Financial Plan. We have witnessed "austerity" in the European crisis where payments are suddenly reduced. This is a Plan-Based Investing nightmare as you have little warning and a sudden need for increased income from your investments.

> **The "illions" risk.** *Million* sounds like *billion* which sounds like *trillion*. Soon we use the terms interchangeably with little

thought to the exponential differences between them. For a little perspective, consider this: a million seconds last for less than twelve days, whereas a billion seconds last over thirty-one years. *Stop! Holy smokes!* A trillion seconds last over 31,000 years. Guess what? We just fogged over because we can't relate to 31,000 years—and because of that we cannot wrap our minds around being one trillion dollars short of money in the US budget each year—we just can't. Because of that, every cut seems too small to entertain—so we don't cut anything—ever!

Government bond/increased interest-rate risk. If your credit declines, then by definition you are less able to make your payments. When this happens to a government, the government's payments on newly issued bonds are higher, and the government will require a larger percentage of its income to pay the interest on those loans. Eventually you will not be able to borrow at a rate in which you can make the payments. (Or you just won't get credit anymore, ala Detroit) Note: Bonds are loans. The bondholders agree to give you money, and you agree to pay the money back plus the interest you promised when they gave you that money.

Incomplete-reporting risk. This is the fact that the facts are ignored or sugar-coated to keep you in the dark as to the truth. Using Social Security as an example, it is not only the obligation to pay back the money that was already spent on other government programs, it is the obligation to pay future benefits, which will come in at a slower rate due to demographic trends that tell us less people will be paying into the system versus those drawing money out. I have seen this estimate from between fifty and one hundred trillion dollars. Go to www.pgpf.org and begin to get a feel for what I am saying with the facts.

Denial-of-the-truth risk. This is a form of "normalcy bias" where we know, or think we know, how bad it is for our country and many others, but as long as there is someone who says it will all be OK we side and vote for that person. Watch *The Poseidon Adventure* and see how so many people deny common sense while being in an upside-down ship. They assume that the ship's "leadership," who are the experts at piloting the ship, are also the leaders to follow in a disaster. They don't believe it makes sense to go where the water will go last. You won't know the "truth" if you rely on others to identify it for you. Does it seem logical to you that those in charge of our country with 230-plus years of history cannot agree on changes to make to stop a coming financial disaster and implement them? Is it possible that they have a vested interest in hiding the truth?

Trust-the-politician risk. This is politicians asking us to trust them with solving the problems of today that they were a part of creating in years past. You might also call this a job-preservation program.

Political-rhetoric risk. It's the incredibly powerful risk of trying to fix government versus examining how your Financial Plan will be affected by the direction the country is going. I am not smart enough to know how to fix the government's fiscal problems. Plan-Based Investing strategies need to consider that if you don't have a strategy, you will become subject to servitude to those who rescue you, even if they are the same people who created the problem in the first place.

Demographic risk. Maybe the greatest risk to your life and the prices of nearly everything. Harry Dent and his company have made an entire business on the study and the application of the data of our demographic trends and our spending and savings habits. Ignore at your own peril. Check it out at: www.harrydent.com.

Lesson Twelve: *The majority of these risks may never be defined anywhere but in this book. That does not make them any less true.*

The "New Economy" risk. My bias is no doubt evident. I am concerned about the future financial stability of our country and the world. We don't know for sure what a collapse of our government or other major economies in the world will look like or how it will play out. If your Financial Plan and your Financial Strategies don't address this issue, then you should ask why you are with your current Advisor. They suffer from a variety of the risks I have defined above. An Advisor in times of normalcy may not be the Advisor you need to follow when times are anything but normal.

Sudden change risk. This is an outcome of many of the risks mentioned previously coming true and the fact that the result may be a sudden change in what we have come to know as "normal."

We tend to examine problems from the top down, government down to people. What if we changed our perspective and looked at them from a person's perspective? If you now work and receive health insurance without a contribution on your part, do you understand the cost? If you are asked to contribute 10 percent of that cost without an increase in your pay, you will need to adjust your spending in other areas of your life to keep your budget in balance. Is it your fault that you did not have this extra money in your budget? Building an investment strategy or set of strategies that can react to changes, whether they are sudden or gradual, is a key component to Plan-Based Investing.

Ponzi-financing risk. To explain this risk, I'll quote Daniel Stelter co-author of "Accelerating out of the Great Recession: How to win in a slow growth economy"

> *Hedge financing,* in which the debtor has sufficient cash flow to pay interest and to pay back the principal.

> *Speculative financing,* in which the debtor can service the loan—that is, he or she can pay the loan interest that is due but not repay the principal out of income cash flows. Therefore, the debtor needs to continuously roll over liabilities by contracting new debt in order to meet the obligations on maturing debt.

> *Ponzi financing* is financing in which the debtor doesn't have enough cash flow to cover either the principal or the interest. While hoping that the asset will rise faster in value than the total financing cost, he or she must borrow even more to meet the interest payments. The ultimate goal is to be "bailed out" by selling the asset to the next buyer.[1]

Makes you think, doesn't it?

I understand that this is not a complete or exhaustive list of all risks associated with the Financial Planning process. It is primarily made up of risks you may have forgotten about—or more likely, have never even thought about. The risks may seem amusing or downright funny; your Advisor may consider them ridiculous, but that will not make them any less true. Choosing who to follow and what they are willing to tell you about the journey in advance would definitely help you choose an Advisor.

---

1 "Ending the Era of Ponzi Finance: Ten Steps Developed Economies Must Take," with contributions from Ralf Berger, Jendrik Odewald, and Dirk Schilder. Referenced in an e-mail from John Mauldin in his January 4, 2013, letter entitled, "Outside the Box." (For more, see www.mauldineconomics.com.)

The insurance sales profession has used visualization to help you realize the problems you will have after a noninsured disaster for as long as insurance has been sold. Is that wrong? Isn't it their job to point out the potential costs to you in the event of a noncovered loss to help you with the decision of buying insurance?

Is it unethical for me to use the potential of disaster to move you forward to a Financial Plan design that will ultimately lead you to how to invest?

Have these risks always existed? Is it possible that there is a greater likelihood of some disasters occurring today than ever before in our life or the life of our country?

Can an investment plan be credible that does not consider the risk of economic and financial upheaval?

Can a Financial Advisor or your source of financial advice be credible if they don't consider that same possibility?

CHAPTER FIVE

Accountability

Expectation is a word that sends shockwaves through the mind of all Financial Advisors. But why? The simple answer is that it's impossible to reliably predict the outcome of variables you can't control. Nothing remains fixed or the same forever, so failure-proof predictions are impossible. Many have tried to provide a level of predictability by merging science and probability, but such a method still needs historical repetition, and history is not about to be repeated in a short-term, predictable pattern.

Lesson Thirteen: *Let me give you a bit of industry-insider information. Advisors in the US financial planning industry are overseen by a governmental agency. These regulators inspect our offices, examine our correspondence to our clients, oversee advertising, and provide us with a list of things you cannot do or say. They are not particularly fond of words such as "guarantee" or "projections" because these words can be perceived to guarantee a successful outcome. No matter who your Advisor is or what your plan is, a successful outcome <u>cannot be guaranteed.</u>*

This reality makes "accountability" a bit of a tricky concept. I hope you are still with me because here's a critical point I don't want you to miss:

- **Accountability of process** *should be* guaranteed.
- **Accountability of reporting** *should be* guaranteed.
- **Accountability of tracking** *should be* guaranteed.
- **Accountability of results** *should be* guaranteed, too—*but it can't be.* The world simply has too many variables. However, if the other three "accountabilities" are guaranteed, you will know where you stand as you progress toward your goals.

Got it?

You can use the first three "accountabilities" to test your source of investment advice.

Does your source of investment advice have a process of how he or she builds Financial Plans, reports to you, and tracks your progress toward your desired outcome? If he or she doesn't, then is it a source of advice that you can rely upon? Remember, your source may be a person or any other source of information. Is it wise to rely upon advice or information where the provider of this information is not accountable to have a process or to follow it?

If you are thinking "but I like her" or "I don't want to hurt her feelings" or "but my friends go to her," then I need to be blunt: you will probably never achieve the success you want because you are not willing to do the things necessary to achieve it. Sorry, I would like to sugarcoat that idea, but I thought that at this moment in the book we are getting to know each other a bit.

Let me give you an example in the world of sports. I bleed green and gold as a lifelong fan of the Green Bay Packers and football as a game. On the professional level, it is often the job of management and the coaching staff to make a tough decision that involves releasing or trading away a person who has been key to past success. The question for the leadership team cannot be what have they done for us; it needs to be what can they do to contribute to our future success. Choosing your reliable source of financial information is similar in that what has gotten you to where you are today may not be what is best to get you to the next level. The Plan-Based Investing strategy is a logical Financial Planning strategy. It may not be how you have arrived here today, but it may be the key to a future of goal accomplishment.

Remember, it does not matter how much you are paying for the advice you receive if the provider does not follow the very simple "guarantees of accountability." You may be paying $14.95 for a financial magazine or $5,000 for a Financial Plan—it is always too much if there is not accountability for the advice.

Let me dig into the three areas of "accountability" that I outlined earlier in the chapter and how they relate to a relationship with an "Advisor" that happens to be a paid professional.

"Accountability of reporting" has to do with how you receive information about your investments and/or your financial progress toward your Financial Plan goals. Let's start with the minimum so you know the lowest level of reporting available. Statements generated from the investment or an insurance company sent through the mail is the minimum level of reporting. If you are receiving this level of reporting, it could indicate many things. It could indicate to you that your Advisor does not have a way to examine all of your investments in a comprehensive, consolidated way. It may even indicate what he or she thinks of you. It may indicate that you negotiated the fee so low your Advisor doesn't have time to service you because you are asking him or her to do something and are not willing to pay for it. It is tempting to bash the level of service you are receiving as inadequate. It may be inadequate or it may only be what you signed up to receive. I believe it makes sense to receive your investment information in a manner that allows you to track it toward your goals. That leads us the next area of Advisor accountability.

"Accountability of tracking" is comparing your investment reports to your goals, which can be done in a variety of ways. The idea is to give you an indication of how you are progressing toward your goal accomplishment. This is the basis for meetings with your Advisor. Either you are on track to accomplish your goals or you are not. If you are not, are you close enough to them that no changes need to be made, or do you need to make investment changes? I will now need to digress again to point out one of the savage deficiencies of the investment industry.

Many of you still think you have a Financial Plan, but all you have is an investment allocation plan. There is a stark difference between the two. Investing is critical, but so are insurance coverage, a college-funding strategy for your children, an auto-purchase strategy, and an estate strategy. If your Advisor has never even asked about these items, he or she is not a Plan-Based Advisor, and you need to fire your Advisor and find a Plan-Based Advisor to oversee your Financial Plan.

Someone needs to be held accountable to track your progress toward your goal! If not your Advisor—you!

"Accountability of process" can be a bit trickier than the accountability of reporting or the accountability of the tracking of your investment progress against your goals. You may trust the Advisor you work with to have an "accountability of process." If your Advisor has not described the process of how he or she does business, the best idea I can share with you is to ask.

"Process" in the context of this chapter refers to your Advisor's financial planning process in regard to how you are serviced. How often do you meet? What are the expectations of the meeting? How are you progressing toward your goals? How does he or she choose investments for you to invest into? Your Advisor should also have a system of checking your tax strategy by reviewing your returns and discussing your strategy—or creating one. How often are goals reviewed? What insurance do you have? What are the limits? Do you have any new heirs to add as beneficiaries? And so on and so on and so on.

You should be meeting regularly with your Advisor.

- You should know why you are meeting.
- You should walk away feeling the "why" was answered.
- You should know when you'll meet again.

- You should know where you stand when you leave. If your Advisor is a Plan-Based Advisor, you should know your progress toward your planned goals.

Here are some other "accountabilities" that your Advisor should adhere to:

- Accountability of due diligence—is she or he doing regular research?
- Accountability to common sense. Enough said.
- Accountability to God—this will help keep your Advisor in check, but it is not a guarantee. We are all sinners.

You may be handling your own financial affairs without using an Advisor. For you the same criteria previously outlined can be used by you to design, implement, and monitor your own Financial Plan. It is tempting to shortcut the process, but like anything done right, it is hard work. Done right, with proper processes in place, the entire process produces a magical momentum and peace of mind you will not have if you know nothing about your financial destiny.

CHAPTER SIX

Why "Plan-Based Investing"?

Why not?

Lesson Fourteen: *With all of the information available today versus fifty years ago, we have not seen a dramatic improvement in the percentage of people who are financially successful. When I say "why not," I mean it. A common denominator of success is a vision of success and a plan to achieve it.*

The "low-fee" industry is a fairly new industry. You can buy or sell a stock for the price of a cup of coffee. You are able to identify a significant amount of research information about investments online at no cost at all. Consumers are able to compare investments and to look back in time to see how they reacted in various market conditions. These are incredible tools and advantages for today's investors.

Why hasn't this improved the numbers of those who are investments successes?

The financial industry players are primarily product pushers who are not held accountable for results. Bluntly put, they are "profiteers" who push for industry standards that defend their status quo. The "big players" with lots of assets will push standards and rules that allow them to service a lot of people with corporate, broad-based advice. They will defend "low fees" as the measurement because they have them, and they need a large base of people to pay them to create profit for their companies. They are not held accountable for results. They are motivated by asset gathering and will do anything to gather more, and that may be at the cost of your financial future.

They are the result of an industry that had its eye on the wrong ball. If low fees were the sole determinant of success, then everyone with a low-fee, low-trading-cost account should be successful. I hope you read that again and realize the sheer stupidity of that thought pattern. If a five-star rating were the determinant of success, then why doesn't everyone with five-star funds find success? If proper allocation is the sole determinant, then... You get the idea.

Turn on CNBC or Bloomberg TV, and you will see ads that feature just that—top performance, low fees, research capabilities, stocks versus currencies, green lines, five stars, and so on. You'll see everything except a "Personal Financial Plan with goal-tracking and accountability." Seriously, do you think derivatives and their use in your mutual funds are the reason for your success? Is the value of the euro or the dollar going to determine which fund allocation you choose in your 401(k)? Do you care that the average duration of the PIMCO Total Return Fund Institutional Class is 4.73 years as of March 31, 2013? Do you even know why that is important? (You probably have it in your 401(k), if you have one.) Listen to the radio and hear about gold and silver. Open a financial magazine and read how fees detract from your return.

Are they serious? Most of this garbage is important only to a very few people. Yet it appears everywhere. Why? Primarily to impress you that they know of this minutia.

You Need a Financial Plan!

It needs to provide a map to where you are going! You need to have an insurance strategy and a plan! You need to have a tax strategy and a plan! You need to have an investment strategy and a plan! You need to save an enormous percentage of your income, and saving may require a significant sacrifice to your current lifestyle. You need to work with someone who understands the previous five points for accountability.

Your Financial Plan needs to dictate why you insure and invest and how you insure and invest. It must dictate how you track what you insure and invest and how often you track and monitor and adjust your progress toward your goals. It must determine how much to save, how to save it, and what you do when you are not on track to meet your goals. It should determine what strategies you will use toward the accomplishment of your goals. Seriously, you need all of this stuff to start getting serious about your future. I know the large financial pornography outlets don't care if you do or you don't. Their goal is to sell advertising to make money to please their shareholders.

You Need A Plan-Based Investing Strategy

I call it "Plan-Based Investing"—and I also call it common sense—because it cuts through the constant babble of financial pornography babblers and goes straight to your personal plan for success.

It is really that simple?

You also need to read the next chapter as I try to scare you into learning what facts are important by taking a macro view of the world in which we live.

Note: Fees are important; so is research and the duration on your bond holdings. My point is that I believe it is more important to understand the motive of *why* someone is promoting one key idea over another. Investing based on the goals of your personal Financial Plan passes the "Yes, that makes sense" test much more than any one of those aforementioned items. Once you assemble your investment vehicles to complete your Financial Plan, the items I have poked fun at will all be important. When I grew up, my grandparents often used the phrase "Don't put your cart in front of your horse." I translate this to mean "Don't begin your investment program without having your Financial Plan in place. It is the Financial Plan that will tell you how to invest to accomplish that plan."

CHAPTER SEVEN

Wake Up and Look Around at What Is Going On—Then Take Control

Our nation's debt is accelerating—it is out of control with no one willing to sacrifice a life in politics to build a consensus for a change in the way we do business. In testimony before the Committee on the Budget on June 3, 2009, Federal Reserve Chairman Ben Bernanke said, "The recent projections from the Social Security and Medicare trustees show that, in the absence of programmatic changes, Social Security and Medicare outlays will together increase from about 8½ percent of GDP today to 10 percent of GDP by 2020 and 12.5 percent by 2030. With the ratio of debt to GDP already elevated, we will not be able to continue borrowing indefinitely to meet these demands. Addressing the country's fiscal problems will require a willingness to make difficult choices." Let me translate. If these areas of the government take a larger and larger share, something else has to shrink. What might that be? Or worse yet, how much faster will debt grow when we are unwilling to cut anything?

You can search www.ssa.gov for "Trustee Report Summary" and read the current report. Grab a cold beverage before you sit down because you will be shocked by the warnings you have probably never heard about.

That alone should scare you. If it doesn't, you may be a victim of the dumbing-down-of-Americans tactic. Isn't it interesting how "trillions" sounds like "billions"? We are being told that we can fix our problems without sacrifice if we can get the other guy to pay more. You may want to reread chapter 4 about risk to refresh your mind. Reread the "illions risk."

We (the people of the United States of America) are a country with two and a half trillion dollars of income from those of us who pay income taxes. Our country's obligation to future users of our health-care system, retirement system, and the holders of our debt is somewhere north of seventy trillion dollars ($70,000,000,000,000). This includes our current debt and the future obligation to pay Social Security benefits and government pensions and to provide health care to government employees and servicemen and -women along with Medicare and Medicaid benefits. That is a tough ratio of income to debt—a mess no matter how you slice it.

If you believe that history repeats itself, then you need to believe that when it does, the circumstances are similar. We are accelerating at an exponential pace toward a point at which we cannot disguise the problem. Many have their opinions as to where the breaking point of our economy lies, but no one knows for sure; at least there does not seem to be a consensus. *But that is not the point!* When we all wake up and look behind the curtain—as in *The Wizard of Oz*—we will see that our current course is one of certain failure.

Why Discuss Our Country's Future Financial Headwinds?

The Financial Plan is yours, and if you, your Financial Plan, or your Advisor are oblivious to the facts surrounding our country's financial future, you are doomed to follow the masses to where the masses will go. Generally speaking, the masses don't do well as long as they remain a part of the mass. I have some very strong opinions about the politicians who promise to dig us out but who were parts of the team who buried us in the first place. Those opinions aside, however, the strategy here is not about how to change the problem—it is about how to interpret it and use that information to build your Financial Plan. Understanding how change may play out will help you with your Plan-Based Investing.

You need to recognize macro trends and build a strategy to react to the continuous political mess. Most people are entrenched in their political views—hopefully your Advisor is not and can see the big picture no matter who is in charge. You want someone who can build a plan that prepares you no matter how the political pendulum swings.

Please go to www.pgpf.org and read what David Walker, a former comptroller general of the United States, has to say about where the United States really and truly stands today.

Please also read *Endgame: The End of the Debt Supercycle and How It Changes Everything* by John Mauldin and Jonathan Tepper. This book is a game changer because it brings the world's financial standing into focus. Let me quote a few insights directly from the book: "Everyone knows we are on an unsustainable path of spending, yet not enough politicians have the foresight, let alone the courage, to do anything about it, with some notable exceptions" (p. 82). Later, still referring to the United States, they write, "When people suddenly and unexpectedly lose faith in the U.S. debt, we will not see a slow increase in interest rates and a slow decline of the dollar. We will be unlikely to have time to take the right steps. By that stage, it will be too late. The decline will happen quickly and unexpectedly" (p. 188).

In light of all that, now consider your own personal investment strategy or the one being used by your Advisor to handle your life savings. While none of us desires disaster in any facet of our lives, it makes sense to have a plan should it occur. It should be a part of a Plan-Based Investing strategy. How are you prepared to act when this upheaval happens?

How will you change your current strategy, and where will you go with your investment allocation? In the book referenced above, I quoted the words "quickly and unexpectedly." Those are game-changer words. They may incite panic when you think of how you are currently investing.

In the past, how have you changed your investment allocation? Was it in response to changes in market conditions? Were the changes you made discussed in the past as an alternative plan of action that you then implemented? Are you prepared to react with your investment portfolio in the event of a financial meltdown?

A large problem with the decline of our worldwide solvency is trying to wrap our arms around the timing of when these events will affect our lives and our investments. Are our decisions based on the reality of the situation or mere perceptions? When and how does this threaten our investment strategy?

What Next?

You are now informed—so it's time to schedule a meeting with your Financial Advisor to check in on his or her worldwide view and strategy for you. If you are handling your own Financial Plan, then you need to do the same—establish your disaster strategy.

Take Control—My Disaster Strategy

I believe in tactical and rotational investment strategies.

I believe that buy-and-hold investments are best when it is the only strategy available as is true in most 401(k) plans. (Yes, fees are important with buy-and-hold strategies.)

I believe in the wisdom of knowing in advance of alternatives you will consider in the event of an event that will negatively affect your investments.

I know that no one strategy will or can always be in favor and producing to a level that we desire.

Why do I believe in tactical and rotational investment strategies? Both of these investment strategies give someone authorization to reposition assets. In my experience a change is not made in anticipation of events that could affect the market. That would be market timing and considered a game of fool's gold. Rather, it is reacting to indicators that point to a sell signal in one area of your portfolio and a buy signal in another. There are tactical investment strategies where "shorting" an area of the market may be an alternative option. Shorting the market offers the potential to profit from a decline in that sector of the market or a particular security.

Don't write or text me about individual products or sectors that will protect in these circumstances. *I don't care,* because nothing—I mean nothing—is good enough all the time for me to be in it all the time. (Yes, I like hard assets. Yes, I like real estate.) This means I need to have a strategy for when to get in and when to get out.

Your Advisor may say they believe in "active "or "passive" investments. They may believe that "buy and hold" is the best because it is the least expensive. They may tout the "Modern Portfolio Theory" as the basis for their investment. They may use a combination of them. Truth is I am an advocate of all of them at exactly the correct time; the problem is we don't know that time until that time as passed. If you utilize the Plan-Based Investing Strategy and you know what return you need, then the investments you invest in or the strategy you use will depend on the historic data of that strategy. How did the strategy perform in the down markets of 2000-2002 or 2008? How did it perform in the bull markets of 2003 or 2009? At your age and at this stage of your financial life can you afford a 2008 and still accomplish your financial goals?

My statements preceding this may be the reason your Advisor has not recommended this book to you. (It may be why he or she did, if your Advisor has come to the same conclusions I have.)

We are all easily convinced of reasons to make changes in our lives. The hardest part is accepting that what you see is what you see and moving forward with change. I hope at this point in this book you have been given some ammunition to question the status quo with common-sense questions. I believe the examples should motivate you to make some changes or to examine and lay out your Financial Plan, which will lead you to a Plan-Based Investing strategy.

CHAPTER EIGHT

Conclusion

People don't achieve what they hope for. They achieve what they plan for.

Lesson Fifteen: *There is something that happens internally when you complete and implement a Financial Plan. It is a "Peace of Mind" in doing what you know deep inside is the right thing to do.*

A Financial Plan is critical to success. This is especially true in a world of dying pensions, reduced employer match, and a cutback in employer benefits.

You are responsible for your financial success. Really!

There will always be those in society who cannot care for themselves. It is critical that all of us support them and help train them to help themselves.

Insurance is necessary to protect loved ones and maintain a standard of living that they have come to expect.

We are all actors in a play called life. Unfortunately this causes us to create false aspirations to achieve the panacea of a false life of bliss rather than a life of gratification.

We cannot afford the country we live in. Either our costs are too high or our revenue is not sufficient or both. America is under attack internally and externally, and most Advisors are blind to the impact these attacks are likely to have on normal, historic investing—suddenly.

We will always complain about those in charge and the decisions they make. Working with an Advisor who prepares for the potential fallout of those decisions is critical.

Debt is bad. Please don't get sucked into justification as to why it is good.

Taxes destroy investment returns.

Inflation erodes investment returns (and completely eliminates them in some cases).

Inflation can be used to your advantage with fixed-rate debt and will be a disadvantage with fixed-rate income.

If you want something for nothing, someone needs to do something for nothing, which is a cycle that will not grow a society. Pay for superior advice from masters of their craft. You won't regret it.

In the words of John D. Rockefeller, "Don't be afraid to give up the good to go for the great."

Run your life (and that of your family) as if it were a business with income and expenses. Establish a system of examining expenses to seek out lower-cost alternatives on a regular basis.

Prepare an investment disaster plan. Predetermine what your options are with all of your investments, including your work retirement plan.

I believe above all that if you don't have a Financial Plan, then you don't have a way to gauge your progress toward your goals, which means any advice you receive to continue on your current path from any Advisor is malpractice. (This is a *big*, profound point. Reread it a few times.)

From time to time, we all get a dump-truck load of "it" dumped in our laps. Getting out of the rough patches is not easy, but the determining factor of your life's success is how you handle it—in your actions, with your God, and in your plan to overcome and accomplish your dreams from where you are today rather than where you think you should be. Take comfort in that most people are incompetent at achieving financial success. They are good actors and are likely living beyond their means—maybe not every day, but certainly in a lifestyle that cannot be maintained for life. Our government runs its finances the same way.

Life is not easy. Happiness in a free society needs to be tied to our contributions in perpetuating that free society. If you desire happiness, then go to work, pay your taxes, and contribute a notable percentage of your income and time to those who are not as blessed as you are. This book was not written to be a Shakespearian masterpiece. It was written to point out shortcomings of the financial services industry and why it is time to change the discussion. We are all individuals with individual and unique aspirations for our life. It seems logical to build a personal Financial Plan that is not rigid but will be changed based on your changing dreams and goals. It is logical to build an investment strategy based on the goals of your personal Financial Plan. It makes sense to review it regularly. It certainly makes sense to find and trust a partner that can provide benefits to you beyond their cost.

It's called "Plan-Based Investing." And I believe it is the description of the future in investing.

Further Reading

www.dankennedy.com   If you are in business—you need Dan.

www.briantracy.com   I recommend the book *Goals!*

www.bobmcewen.com   Order the *Politics—Easy as Pie* video.

www.socialsecurity.gov   Search for "Trustee Report Summary."

www.pgpf.org   Click on "Fiscal Outlook."

www.cfp.net   Click on "Financial Plan Basics."

www.mauldineconomics.com   Sign up for the newsletters.

www.harrydent.com   Sign up for the newsletters.